# Love bugs

MW00899997

by Nina Benedetto

# Welcome to the enchanted world of Love bugs:

Where children are loved and supported as they learn life's lessons. These magical beings show parents and caregivers how to help children become ready, willing and able to be self-motivated, cooperative and respectful.

In this land, the Love bugs see situations from the children's point of view. Love bugs love and accept all children just as they are. What shines right out of them is pure unconditional love, understanding and acceptance. Love bugs show us how to be our children's advocates rather than their critics.

The power of the Love bugs comes from their ability to remain completely on each and every child's side, even when [especially when] a child is 'in trouble'. Instead of a system that rewards or punishes certain behaviors,

## Love bugs ONLY notice how children make the world more wonderful!

The Love bugs want children to do the right things for the right reasons, but they do not tell them what to do. Love bugs trust that with guiding, supportive questions from adults, children have the ability to investigate problems and discover solutions.

**A cautionary note:** Love bugs are a powerful tool for encouraging parents to accept each child exactly where they are. Telling children that the Love bugs are disappointed or displeased will "squash" the magic of the Love bugs. Love bugs do not give approval or disapproval - **EVER!** Nor do they expect children to impress them in any way.

## May you celebrate many magical moments together.

On the day you are born—magical beings called Love bugs begin to cherish you!

The best thing about love bugs is that every day they only

notice
all of
the
ways

♩ ♩ ♪ ♪ ♩ ♪♩ ♪♪

You make
life more
wonderful!

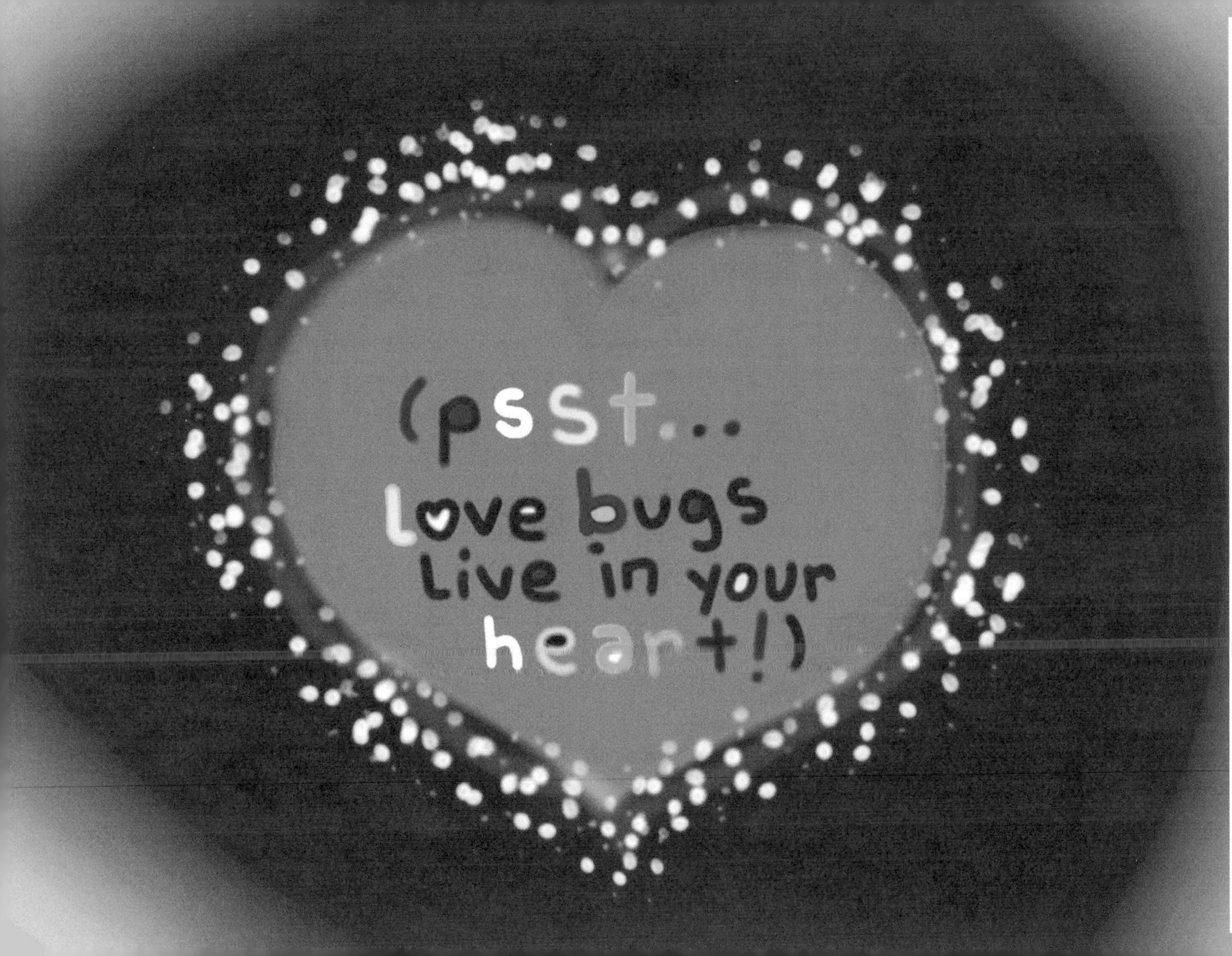
(psst...
love bugs
live in your
heart!)

You know what?

If you have a hard day,

get grouchy,

or down in the dumps

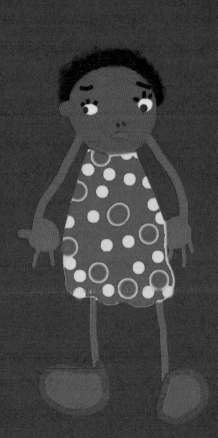

Love bugs keep you company . . .

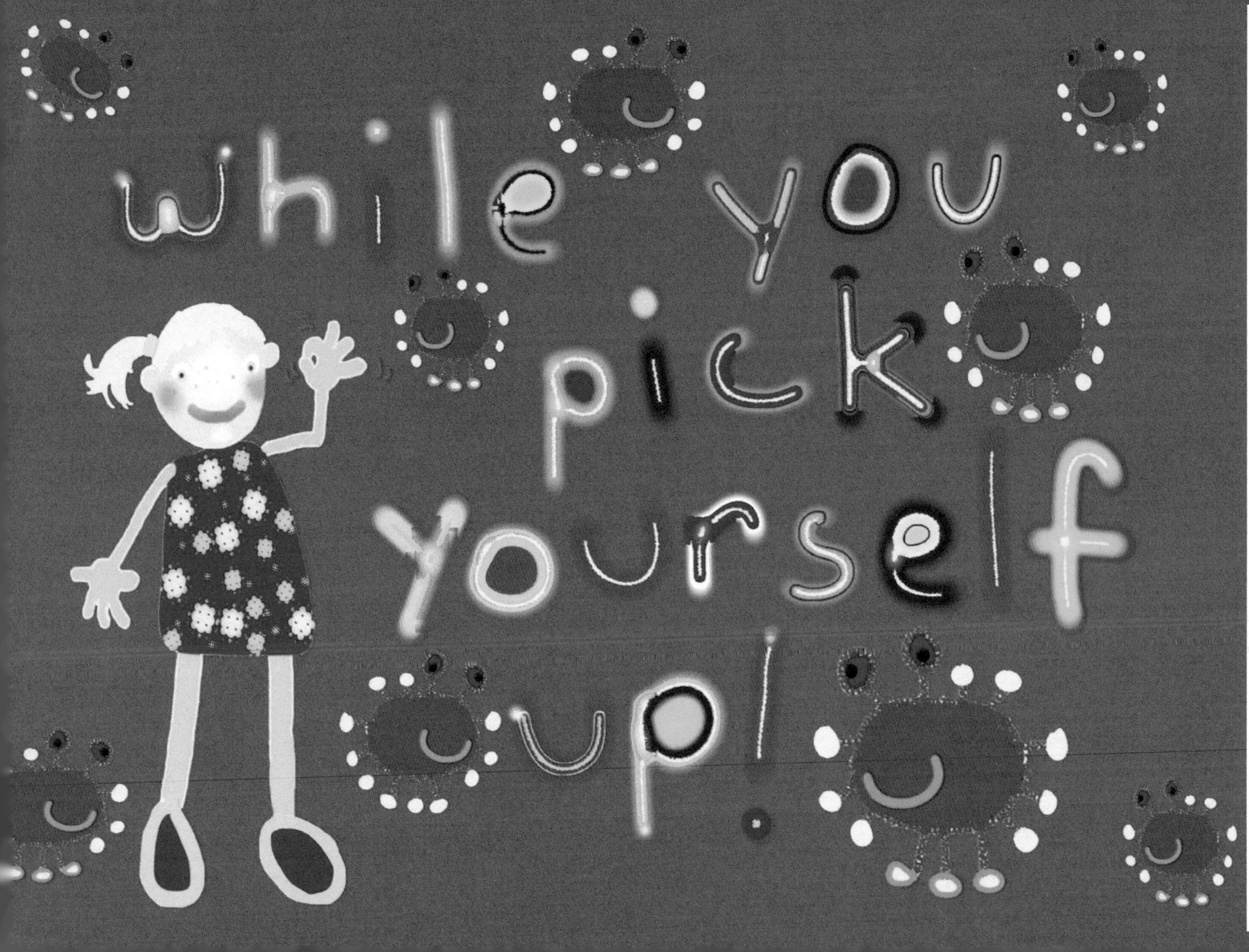
while you pick yourself up!

If you do something wrong — or get in trouble...

love bugs
do not fuss,
scold or
punish...
instead

Love bugs begin to buzz zzz and cheer for you to find a more wonderful way!

Love bugs stay by your side... and on your side!

YOU

KNOW

WHY?

Love bugs are certain that... you learn from mistakes

you know...

love bugs never tell you what to do, because

Love bugs always ...... always believed in you!

In your
darkest
moments...

and

your

sunniest

days →

of course...

you will find

your own

way!

the

beginning

I wonder how you know that the Love bugs are always on your side?

I wonder what you would want the Love bugs to notice?

I wonder

how it

feels...

...to have
Love bugs
in your
heart?

A Parent's Guide/How to be a 'Love bug' and truly be on your child's side. Being a 'Love bug' is not easy! The strategies are simple but difficult to do well.

But guess what? Beyond the limitations of our patience, good humor, and energy children need us to be on their side.

The best thing about being a Love bug is... THAT: Every day instead of using manipulation in order to control children, we become their life coaches!

And you know what? Because of that, they become ready, willing and able to learn self-motivation, respect, and co-operation!

# Here's how:

Notice a child's positive actions by describing what you see, hear, and feel instead of giving praise. Describe how his or her actions affect you: "Thank you for putting the dirty clothes in the hamper! Now I get to enjoy a tidy bathroom." [Instead of just saying "Good job."] "I hear you asking for a turn in a sweet voice. I feel happy when I see you treating your brother with respect." [Instead of just saying "Good boy."] "You cleaned up the living room! Now I can relax!" [Instead of just saying "I am proud of you."]

Find many ways to say thank you:
-for helping
-for the hug

-for being my daughter/son
-for remembering to feed the dog

List and PROMINENTLY display all acts of kindness:

**You let your brother have the first turn!**

**When you see trouble coming, let your child know that you see the situation from his or her point of view:** "You look upset. Did you want that toy?"

Accept your child's reasons: **[Often he or she is doing the wrong thing for the 'right' reasons - at least as he or she sees it.]** "Did you hit her because she wouldn't let you have a turn?" [I want it!] "I bet you felt angry!" [She made me mad!] "You did not like that." [No, I didn't!]

**Then ask probing questions:** "Were you trying to teach her a lesson?" [YES!] "Hmmm... so, let's think about this. If she hit YOU, would it make you want to give her a turn?" [OH!] "Can you find a better way to get a turn?" [Use my words?]

Ask guiding questions: "Do you think she is finished?" [She is taking a long time!] "Could you ask her for a turn when she is all done?" [When you are all done, can it be my turn?]

**Back both children up in case the other child also needs support in learning to take turns. If the other child refuses the request, then support his or her feelings. Allow both children to feel their feelings - especially the difficult ones:** "Are you finished?" [I'm not done!] "I know it hurts when you want a turn right now! It is hard to wait."

"I know, I know, you really want it! It is hard to take no for an answer!"

PERSUADING or DISSUADING doesn't work: Every human being is convinced of his or her own viewpoint. Attempting to 'sell' a child on your truth forces that child to cling harder to his or her own. It is not always possible to avoid persuading or dissuading your child into doing the 'right' thing. Unfortunately, a child may become oppositional in response to your advice or logic. Instead of trying to convince or manipulate a child into following your way, it is more effective to encourage him or her to find a way that works. This support for a child's important work of finding better solutions develops in them the ability to solve problems.

**Avoid criticism, complaints or punishment:** Ask or tell your child what you would like from him or her. "Be gentle." [Instead of "Do not hit your little brother!"] "Be more responsible." [Instead of "You forgot!"] "I like to be asked nicely." [Instead of 'Do not yell at me!" [or even "Say please."]

'**Love bugs**' are the distillation of everything I have learned about child development, teaching, parenting, relationships, motivation, communication and compassion that, when practiced, make the world more wonderful for children and the adults who cherish them.
For more stories that open hearts and minds, please visit my website at:
www.wonderwisdombooks.com

Made in the USA
Charleston, SC
13 September 2015